Songwriting

Step by Step

Aaron Cheney

Moonlight Garden
Publications
Renton, Washington

No part of this book may be used or reproduced by any means, graphic, electronic, or mechanical, including photocopying, recording, taping or by any information storage retrieval system without the written permission of the publisher except in the case of brief quotations embodied in critical articles and reviews.

Copyright 2011, Aaron Cheney. All rights reserved.

Cover art by Aaron Cheney.
Edited by S. C. Moore.

ISBN: 978-1-938281-24-2   Paperback Large Print
Library of Congress Control Number: 2023931771

Large Print Edition published in 2023
by Moonlight Garden Publications,
an imprint of Gazebo Gardens Publishing, LLC.
www.GazeboGardensPublishing.com

Printed in the United States of America.

For Katherine, Jeff, and Jessica.

Table of Contents

INTRODUCTION		5
CHAPTER ONE:	Tools Of The Trade	9
CHAPTER TWO:	Getting Creative	20
CHAPTER THREE:	Writing Great Lyrics	34
CHAPTER FOUR:	Crafting Great Music	71
CHAPTER FIVE:	You've Got A Song	95
APPENDIX		122
SONG CHECKLIST		123
ACKNOWLEDGEMENT		124
ABOUT THE AUTHOR		125

Introduction

Songwriters (and artists of any ilk, for that matter) are generally divided into two camps: those who wish to approach what they do as an art form regardless of the economic consequences, and those who wish to create within commercial parameters, with the intention of profiting by it. I have attempted to write a book that provides valuable information for both.

After a little thought I decided the best way to begin was by asking the two simple questions below. Take a minute to think about your answers, and what effect they should have on the songs you write.

Why Songwriting?

Though it seems an obvious question, it's important to discuss it for a minute before we get down to work, because the purpose of your songs will dictate the kinds of songs you should write. If you are hoping to market and sell your songs to established artists, there are standards you must follow in terms of song form, length, and subject matter if you want to have a reasonable chance of success. Following the "rules" will also give your songs wider popular appeal.

On the other hand, if you intend to perform your own songs or are simply writing for your own enjoyment, you have more flexibility when it comes to the "rules." Whatever your motivations are, your deepest, most fundamental reason for writing songs should be the thrill of the creative process.

I am a songwriter because I love the satisfaction I get from putting words to music and creating something where once there was nothing. Just as some people enjoy getting lost in a good book and losing all sense of time and place, I enjoy becoming lost in the work of songwriting; musing on a story or melody line until suddenly I come across that perfect combination of ingredients that make the entire song work.

At that moment, everything makes sense—how the verses lead into the chorus; how the hook draws you in; how the bridge moves everything to a new level; the song comes into perfect clarity. There still may be work to do before it is completely finished, but at that one moment the song takes on an existence of its own. I write songs to experience that moment.

Whether you aspire to songwriting as an art form or as a commercial venture (both are worthy goals), keep in mind that great songs are full of honest emotional content and that can only come from truly loving the process of songwriting.

Is Songwriting an Art or a Craft?

Well, which is it? Explaining the difference between the two is a little like explaining the difference between a "sport" and a "game"; there is some gray area. Since this is my book, I'm going to use these definitions: a "craft" is a creative activity that follows a pattern or set of instructions and requires practical skill. "Art" is a creative activity that isn't necessarily bound by any set of rules and expresses something unique with a sense of beauty and truth. Given that, songwriting is clearly both.

Creativity and rules are not mutually exclusive. Songwriting does have rules that can be taught, learned, and followed. They are the fundamental skills that form the basis for thousands of great songs. However, a songwriter can also draw upon his/her experience with the rules and choose to break them. To help shed some light on what I mean, let's look at a different kind of artist: a master painter. He/she has rules that must be followed: the laws of light, color, and perspective for example. However...as an artist, the rules can be broken any time you choose. Take Escher, whose depictions of people climbing endless circular staircases or standing in multiple dimensions have fascinated viewers for years. They distort perspective and trick the eye into believing things that could never exist in the natural world.

These incredible drawings are not the product of mere chance or ignorance. Escher knew the rules of perspective. His adherence to them and years of experience and practice eventually led to a deep understanding, and that understanding led to art. It is understanding that allows you to not just break the rules, but break them brilliantly!

This book is about learning the rules of songwriting in order to gain an understanding of them. It is about learning how to "craft" a song, through rewrites and careful scrutiny, into something unique and artful. Lastly, it's about enjoying the journey of the songwriting process with every song you write.

Chapter One
Tools of the Trade

Just as with any artist or craftsman, songwriters use a certain set of tools in their trade. Standing head and shoulders above them all in importance are these three: A notebook, a rhyming dictionary, and a thesaurus. I can hardly imagine writing a song without them. A close fourth is a dictionary.

Musically speaking, the vast majority of songs are written either on a guitar or piano. Additionally, modern technology has provided songwriters with some new tools such as hand-held recorders and computers. Different songwriters use these tools in different ways and with differing levels of success. Over time you'll find the way that works best for you.

Notebook

Buy yourself a decent notebook, and for the love of everything good in this world...don't get a spiral-bound! They are messy and don't store or stack well. Don't get one that's too small either. Notebooks that are too narrow make writing uncomfortable and also make it difficult to fit one line of your song on one line of notebook paper. I find that the Mead Composition notebook (College Ruled) is perfect for me. It's sturdy, bound with stitches, and just the right size.

Your notebook is your songwriting database. Remember the old saying, "the shortest pencil remembers longer than the longest memory"? It has never been truer than when it pertains to songwriting. Don't ever depend on your brain to remember a good turn of phrase or song idea. Write it down!

The world of music is full of anecdotes about such-and-such an artist writing down the idea for their new hit song on a bar napkin or funeral program, and there is a good reason for it: they understood that an idea that doesn't get written down is in serious jeopardy of being forgotten. Sure, it seems easy enough to remember when it's rattling around up there in your brain, but believe me, it isn't.

Carry your song notebook everywhere, and write an

idea down the minute it comes to you! If you get caught somewhere without it, write your idea down on whatever is at hand (or maybe even on your hand!) and transfer it to your notebook later. You'll thank me. Over the years I've developed a way of writing in my book that seems to work pretty well. First, I write my name and contact info on the first page. (Ever lose your notebook? I have.) Then I flip that page and begin my first set of lyrics on the first right-facing page. This would be page three, for those of you who are following along. I use that page for my lyrics, and the left page (Page 2) for any notes, rhymes, or other thoughts that occur to me as I'm working. For all subsequent songs, I simply follow the same pattern: lyrics on the right, notes on the left. This technique allows me to see my lyrics and my working-notes at the same time, without having to flip pages.

I also keep a running list of title ideas starting on the very last page of my notebook. This is where I jot down any phrases, wordplays, or metaphor ideas I happen to come across. As those ideas begin to fill pages, I work backwards through the notebook. Eventually my lyric pages and my title ideas will meet somewhere in the middle, and it's time for a new notebook. I then file that notebook (I wouldn't dare throw it away!) neatly in with all my other songwriting notebooks (good thing I didn't buy a spiral bound), making sure to label the front of it with a few notes about what's inside. Why? Because filing your notebooks is not about storage, it's about retrieval. Usually about half the song ideas in one of my notebooks haven't had anything done with them yet, and I want to be able to find them again. Old notebooks can also be a great place to go if you're ever stuck for ideas.

Rhyming Dictionary

Using a rhyming dictionary is not cheating. In fact, not using one is just re-inventing the wheel. Why waste time trying to find all possible rhymes for a given word when someone has already done it for you? I suppose some writers find it romantic to imagine their lyrics manifesting themselves in epiphanies of pure creativity. Problem is...it rarely happens. Writing lyrics is work, plain and simple, and I'd rather not spend my energy on something I don't have to.

On the other hand, rhyming dictionaries are not foolproof. Don't expect to just flip yours open and start filling your lyric blanks in with creative and unique words. They aren't always there. Sometimes you'll find words that rhyme but seemingly have no relationship to your lyrics until you make them part of a metaphor. Still other times you'll have to use your own smarts and look up close-rhymes or false-rhymes that can also work for your lyrics. Rhyming dictionaries won't help you come up with conglomerate rhymes either. (More on these later.)

Despite its shortcomings, a good rhyming dictionary is an absolute essential to any songwriter. I recommend The New Comprehensive American Rhyming Dictionary by Sue Young. It categorizes words by sound and includes slang and common phrases.

One last note: there are many great rhyming resources on the Internet now, my favorite being rhymezone.com. You may find them more quick and easy to use than looking up words in a book. I find I prefer something tangible—give me a book any day.

Thesaurus

The third absolute must for songwriters is the thesaurus. Have you ever been stuck trying to cram a word with too many syllables into a line like somebody over-packing a suitcase? Enter the thesaurus! Instantly you have a list of words and phrases with similar meanings that might work in its place. A thesaurus is also a wonderful tool when you want a new way to say something you've heard a million times. Call me weird, but I just love to peruse mine from time to time, trolling for new phrases. I particularly like editions that randomly highlight a group of words and detail the subtle differences in their meanings.

Ever wonder what the differences are between stories, tales, fables, anecdotes, and allegories? I have…and now I know. Choose one that meets your needs, but try to avoid any with the words "travel" or "pocket" in their titles. Roget's is generally considered to be the best, as it is arranged according to the logical flow of ideas.

Dictionary

Along with music, words are the medium of song. As a songwriter, you owe it to yourself to have a wide, working vocabulary. You can't use words you don't know. Even worse, you can misuse a word you only think you know. For a songwriter there is no greater humiliation. When you come across a word you don't know, look it up.

Again, choose a dictionary that meets your needs, but try to avoid any with the words "travel" or "pocket" in their titles. You want a big, fat one with every word you might ever need in it, not some weenie dictionary that's only good for crossword puzzles. Speaking of which…crossword puzzles are another great way to increase your vocabulary. Another great tool is the "word of the day" feature that most Internet service providers offer. Subscribe to it.

As a practicing wordsmith, you should strive to be an avid reader. Reading a wide variety of books will not only expose you to new words, but to new ideas. Words equal power, and powerful words are the lifeblood of powerful lyrics.

Musical Instruments

The guitar is the most popular instrument of our time, and it's not hard to see why; it's easy to learn the basics, very transportable, and musically versatile. An absolute beginner of average ability can learn to strum basic chords in less than a week. I highly recommend having one around even if you don't plan to make it your life's passion. It will give you a quick way to try out whatever you're working on and, if nothing else, look cool sitting in the corner!

The piano is second in popularity. Because of its logical layout, it's quite easy to plunk out melodies and simple chords without much effort. Modern keyboards offer the added benefit of being more portable, and via digital technology are able to approximate the tones of just about any other instrument.

Experienced songwriters will tell you that the instrument you choose to write on will have a profound effect on your songs. People tend to write differently on a piano verses a guitar. Often songwriters will purposely switch between them to break up their songwriting routines and spark some fresh ideas.

If you don't play an instrument, don't despair! Contrary to what you might think, playing one is not prerequisite to being a songwriter. As long as you can communicate what you are hearing in your head to others, you can write songs. Can you hum the tune? That's enough to get started. Ask a friend that plays piano or guitar to help you work out the melody and the chords. That is not to say that the ability to play an instrument and knowledge of music wouldn't be helpful. Just as a large vocabulary will help you write better lyrics, knowledge of theory (the vocabulary of music) will help you write better melodies. Music theory classes are offered at just about every community college. Alternatively, take guitar or piano lessons that include theory as part of the course. The dividends will be well worth the investment.

Recording Devices

Once, long ago, in the 1980's, people used hand-held mini-tape decks to record memos or notes to themselves. They were cool, but the tapes were a hassle and always got lost. Nowadays everything is digital. You can buy a hand-held digital memo recorder for around $50. Many portable mp3 players also have recording capability. They are a godsend for capturing ideas the minute they pop into your mind, and they trump notebooks in one aspect: you can record sound. Carry one around and sing that melody into it before it escapes you.

If you're out-and-about and have a melody you need to capture but no memo recorder, there is another alternative: as E.T. said, "Phone home." I've sung more song ideas into my answering machine than I would care to admit, and my wife always gets a chuckle out of replaying my quirky, off-key, and sometimes rambling "notes-to-self."

Computers

When I first started making music way back in the olden days, the thought of having a recording studio in your home was unheard of, except for the super-rich. Now, thanks to the computer, everybody has one! Who could have ever conceived of a time when you could write, record, design, duplicate, and market your music to the world, all via one little gray box? Software, such as Cakewalk's Sonar and DigiDesign's ProTools, has revolutionized home recording, making it possible for songwriters to write, arrange, and record professional sounding tracks while sitting at home in their pajamas!

A word of warning: writing music on the computer should be approached with caution. It's fine to sing a melody or strum a guitar part into a computer for memory's sake, but resist the temptation to fully record a song until it is written. The allure of the studio, with all its tempting bells and whistles, can be a real song killer! Make sure you stay focused on songwriting and not recording. We'll talk some more on this is Chapter Five.

Writing lyrics on a computer has distinct advantages: your writing is always neat, blocks of text are easy to manipulate and rearrange, and when you're finished, you can easily make multiple copies or email them to someone. Unlike a notebook, however, taking a computer with you everywhere you go is not always easy. Even a laptop can be less than intuitive when you are struck with sudden inspiration. In the time it takes to get it out, boot it up, and open up Word, your idea may be long gone.

For this reason, I still write my lyrics the old-fashioned way. You can bet they'll always end up in a computer, but during the actual writing process I stick with pencil and paper.

After some trial and error you'll find the tools and methods that work best for you. Whatever your approach, the goal is to capture your ideas the instant they occur to you. Sometimes even a thirty second gap between epiphany and preservation is too long!

Chapter Two
Getting Creative

Developing Creativity

The fact that you are even reading this book is enough to know that you are a creative person. For whatever reason, you are driven to manipulate words and notes to build songs. I'd be willing to gamble that you're creative in other mediums as well (drawing or writing perhaps). The success of your songs (and other creative endeavors) over the long term really depends upon your success as an observer and your ability to maintain and nurture your creative spirit. All artists go through "phases" (the Beatles, for example). The way you perceive the world around you is bound to change as you grow and experience new things. Developing your creativity, however, allows you to take advantage of wherever you are in life and turn it into art.

Creativity

It's shocking but true: at its genesis, creativity is simply copying something you like. Artists usually try to candy-coat the fact that their work is based on someone else's with words like "inspiration" and "influence," but it's all the same thing. True artistry, however, is taking that germ of borrowed "inspiration" and augmenting it with something only you can contribute.

Inside you, there are thoughts and ideas garnered from your life experiences that are completely unique and interesting. Learning to recall those things and express them in ways that are both understandable and widely relatable, is what developing your creativity is all about. Many songwriters struggle with finding new ways to express old ideas, but I promise you, that with a little effort, you will be writing lyrics and coming up with new musical ideas that will astound you.

Writing vs. Editing

There are two phases to any artistic endeavor: the creative phase and the analytical phase. For songwriters, that equates to the writing part and the re-writing, or editing part. One of the most valuable things any artist can learn is that these two phases do not work well in tandem. During the writing phase your "creative hat" should be on and all those unique and wonderful ideas inside you should be roaming freely and unchecked.

This kind of creative latitude is only possible if during that same time your "editor's hat" is hanging in the closet behind a rack of old coats. The minute your editor's hat starts to make its way out of the closet and toward your head, you need to stomp on it, kick it, and put it back in the closet. If it tries to come out again, nail it to the wall in the back of the closet and lock the door. It's not the editing hat's turn yet!

During the creative phase you should be writing your ideas down as fast as they come to you, without scrutiny or judgment. Just as a sculptor can't begin his work until he has a lump of clay before him, a songwriter can't begin without a page full of words or musical ideas; so let them come, no matter how silly they seem.

By the way, if they seem silly, it's because your editor's hat has gotten loose again. Give yourself words, lines, notes, and melodies to manipulate before letting that editing hat out of the closet!

Discovering Unique Ideas

Once you've learned which hat to wear and when, you'll find yourself writing things you've never had the courage to write before. Ideas that once seemed too ridiculous to even make the journey from your mind to your pencil will suddenly appear on your paper. These are the very ideas we're after!

At first they may be hard to find, but you can nurture your ability to locate them by writing for a short time every day. Even ten minutes or so of simple prose with no boundaries is enough. Just pick some ordinary object or situation to muse on. No lines. No rhymes. No pressure. Just write. It might help to pick something funny, quirky, or weird the first few times to trick your mind into thinking that what you're writing doesn't matter. Once you become more comfortable writing with only your creative hat on, start going after more serious topics.

As you write, use all your senses: sight, sound, touch, taste, and smell. Your lines will come alive and others will be able to relate to them like never before. Why say, "The attic was dusty," when instead you could say, "Every breath of attic air tasted like a mouthful of dirt." See how much more descriptive the latter phrase is? See how much more quickly and deeply you understand? That's because it hits us all where we live. I mean, let's be honest…who hasn't tasted dirt at least once? The minute a listener hears that line they are immediately taken back to their own dirt-tasting experience, and they understand. They relate to your lyrics on a deeper level.

My family plays a game at reunions that is great for getting to know people, and I've discovered it's also a great idea-generator for songs. Somebody picks an everyday object, and then everyone has to tell a brief personal memory that relates to it. For example, the object might be a pair of shoes. One person might remember standing in Grandpa's big shoes as a child, and someone else might remember playing kickball and their shoe flew off and hit somebody in the face. A third person might remember when mommy chased daddy around the house whacking him with a shoe because he smeared chocolate cake on her face. By the end of an evening, you end up with a big pile of unique and interesting vignettes, and those are what make great songs.

Why write the tired, worn-out "I Love You" chorus when instead you could write about how a husband felt watching his wife put on her makeup, or tucking their children in at night, or standing in the rain waiting for him when he got off work? Sure, Father Mackenzie does weddings down at the church…but it's only when you see him darning his socks in the church all by himself that you really start to understand how lonely he is. (That's from the Beatles song "Eleanor Rigby", by the way...)

The Same Goes For Music

As with lyrics, discovering new musical ideas requires that you discard your editor's hat for a while. A wise guitarist once told me that each time I pick up my guitar to practice, before I play a scale or even warm up, I should play something I've never played before—just a few notes or a phrase that my fingers don't know by rote.

The reason is obvious: as humans we tend to fall into patterns and habits that are familiar and comfortable. We're like the bobcat or the badger at the zoo, following the same circuit through our pen until we've worn a path in the ground. As a person looking in from the outside, we just want to shout, "Snap out of it you silly badger! For once, just turn right instead of left!"

As you write your songs, practice turning right once in a while. Finding something unique requires us to alter our own well-traveled routes and break new ground.

Maintaining Your Creativity

Once you've invested the time in yourself and learned to tap into your unique experiences as a writer, it's important to maintain that creative flow. It's important to realize that some days and some writing sessions will be better than others. Don't be dismayed. There are certain fundamental steps you can take to sustain and heighten your overall level of creativity.

Be Consistent

The most effective thing you can do to maintain your creativity is to be consistent. That same wise guitarist also told me I was better off practicing for fifteen minutes every day than in a two-hour block once a week. Practicing a little everyday leaves less time in between practice sessions for your fingers to forget what they're doing. The same is true for songwriting. A songwriter you should write every single day. If you're strapped for time, even ten minutes is enough. Try not to binge; it saps your energy and gives you an excuse to slack off the next few days. Obviously, some days you'll find yourself "in the zone" and you'll want to take advantage of that state of mind, but never do it at the expense of tomorrow.

When I was a kid a wonderful toy was introduced to the market called Rubik's Cube. I'm sure you're familiar with it. If you're not, it's basically a three-dimensional puzzle. I worked on mine every single day, and after much thought and diligence I managed to solve the top layer. Then something strange happened; I solved the second layer in my sleep! I woke up one morning with the solution in my head, went straight to the Cube, and worked it out as if I had known it all my life. Years later I had a similar experience with a video game called Tetris. In this game you fit geometric shapes together as quickly as you can. After playing it for a few days I found that any time my mind wasn't busy with some conscious thought it was fitting shapes together!

Songs are no different. Putting pen to paper or working on music every day keeps your mind actively engaged in solving the puzzles of songwriting. Most songwriters can tell you of a time or two they have awoken in the middle of the night with a line or phrase in their head. I keep a notepad on my nightstand for just such emergencies, because trust me—you will not remember it in the morning!

Become Prolific

Once you've disciplined yourself to write every day, your song output will naturally increase. This is a good thing, because if you want to write great songs—not good songs, but really great songs—you'll have to write lots and lots of songs. Quality only exists in the midst of quantity, and one great song is usually the byproduct of many good songs. The amazing thing is, as the total number of songs you have written increases, the number of good songs you have to write in between the great ones decreases. Every song is a learning experience that contributes to your total understanding of songwriting.

Occasionally (and by occasionally, I mean virtually never) a great song will come to a songwriter in one brilliant epiphany. When it does, it's only because that songwriter has written many previous songs and made a commitment to remaining constantly immersed in songwriting.

Avoid Writer's Block

The best thing you can do to avoid writer's block is to quit worrying about it. If you assume that you will one day suffer from it, it will become a self-fulfilling prophecy. In my experience, those writers who can't seem to come up with any new ideas have forgotten the most important lesson any artist can learn. Do you remember what it is? That's right… they're trying to wear their "creative hat" and their "editor's hat" at the same time.

Another thing to keep in mind is that trying the same thing over and over will often yield the same result over and over. If you find yourself absolutely stuck, stop thinking like the badger at the zoo and make a right turn instead of the usual left. If you normally write on guitar, try the piano. If you normally write in your living room, try the back yard, or the mountains, or the beach. You need a vacation anyway, right? If you're caught in the middle of a song that's going nowhere, have the courage to discard that idea, and the confidence that a new one will come.

A final word of advice—nothing will kill your creativity deader than staring at a blank page. Never allow yourself to do it! Put something on it…anything! Write the Pledge of Allegiance or "Mary Had a Little Lamb". Doodle. Give yourself some words to start pushing around and get started!

Think Like A Songwriter

One summer my family and I had a chance to go whitewater rafting near Jackson Hole, Wyoming. At one point along the river, our guide told us we were about to enter a series of rapids that would drop us into a calm stretch called "Champagne Canyon." After running the rapids we found ourselves drifting placidly through a deep gorge. Looking down, we noticed the water around us filled with millions of tiny bubbles, creating the illusion that we were indeed floating on an effervescent river of champagne. We asked the guide what made such an interesting phenomenon possible. I won't pretend to remember the answer now, but as you can guess, it had to do with the way the water spilled over the rock formation under the surface, trapping air, and then spitting it out in violent jets that then rose to the surface as tiny bubbles.

As with anyone that enjoys their work, our guide was eager to "talk shop" with us and continued his explanations for the duration of our trip. It was fascinating, and as I listened I came to realize something: where my family and I saw only a beautiful river, our guide saw cause and effect. He knew how the underlying geology would determine the condition of the river. He could identify dangerous formations hiding just below the surface by watching the water move past them. He knew how the river's behavior would change depending on the season and the water level. In short, he was looking at the river through different eyes than my family and I were— the eyes of understanding.

Listen Deeper

This is the way a songwriter should listen to music. It's not enough to dig a song because "it rocks." Ballads shouldn't just "sound pretty." Learn to hear music with new ears. When you listen to something that moves you, ask yourself what is going on under the surface of that song to evoke such a response. What makes it "work"? Why did the songwriter choose this form? Why did he/she forgo a bridge? Why does the last chorus sound so powerful? What makes that particular chord progression evoke such strong emotion? Each question has an answer, and every answer will give you something that can be applied to your own songs.

Sometimes what sells a song is not the songwriting at all. Sometimes a song is carried solely by its production value. Other times it's solely the power of the performance. Being able to recognize a song that doesn't work is valuable too. The more you listen, the more you will recognize that certain techniques bring about predictable results. Once you understand them, you can use them.

Listen To Everything

Do you find rap music insipid? Does country music make you cringe? You should listen to them anyway. Expose yourself to as wide an array of musical styles as possible, even if just for the experience. Music forms such as rock and roll, rockabilly, ragtime, fusion, hip hop, funk, and soul might not even exist had people not been influenced by "outside" music and incorporated it into what they were doing.

Every genre has a unique set of traits that defines it, and being familiar with as many of them as possible will only heighten your ability as a songwriter. What gives a reggae song its characteristic sound, and what differentiates it from ska? Why do the blues sound that way? What sort of language is typical in a rockabilly song? Being fluent in a wide variety of genres will also give you a leg up should you ever be asked to write something outside your comfort zone.

Look Closer

A large part of honing your skill as a songwriter is becoming a keen observer of life in general. Every day you come across hundreds of people, situations, and objects that are the stuff of songs, but they don't present themselves as such; you have to be watching for them. Don't be a casual observer—learn to see past the obvious. Live in the moment and be aware of the world around you.

There is a basic human tendency to only see what you expect to see, even if that is not what you are seeing. Just ask any trial lawyer. It's often worth the effort to be more deliberate in your day-to-day affairs. You'll be surprised.

We are told again and again which car to buy, which clothes to wear, what gas to use, and that life with brand X will be a never-ending party at which every invitee is a super-model. Learn to reject the common media definitions for words like love, success, fun, or beauty. Learn to think for yourself and trust your intuition.

The greatest songs ever written are those that connect with people on a deep, real, profound level. Your songs can do that. You have a lifetime of experiences and viewpoints to draw from. Put forth the effort to find them.

Chapter Three
Writing Great Lyrics

Song Types

Of all the thousands and thousands that have been written, there are basically only three types of songs. Here they are, along with a brief description and some example titles of each:

The "Story" song. Yep, you guessed it: the story song tells a story. "Rocky Raccoon", "Little Red Corvette", "Billy Jean", "The Gambler"

The "Situational" song. This type of song is a story song in disguise. Rather than telling the story as the characters are engaged in it, it tells their back-story by describing the situation they now find themselves in. "Open Arms", "The Search is Over"

<u>**The "Expressive" song**</u> does not tell a story. Instead it offers a state of mind. "Dust in the Wind", "We're Not Gonna Take It", "Annie's Song"

Generally you don't think too much about which category the song you're working on falls into…your song just exists as it first occurred to you. Sometimes, however, it's worth it to "re-imagine" your story song as a situation song, or your situation song as an expressive song. Doing so may spark a new idea that helps it go someplace you might never have thought of otherwise.

Poems vs. Lyrics

Before I say anything more, I want you to read through the two sets of words below. One is a poem and one is a lyric. Can you tell which is which?

Here's the first set:

> With you at the diner working
>   from nine until seven,
> And me working nights at the factory
>   and quitting at dawn,
> It's lucky for me to be home
>   when you leave in the morning,

I try to be early but most days
    you're already gone.
So I crawl into bed, I can smell your perfume,
I can still feel the warmth where you lay,
And it kills me inside to be living our lives
    this way.

We're like the moon chasing the sun,
Somehow we've become intimate strangers.
And as the stars fade in the light,
We both know it ain't right to be alone
    every night
Like intimate strangers.

You'll be home by now,
Reading the note that I left you.
But, "Darling I love you," was all I could
    think of to say.
Because I miss you much more than
    four words can explain,
And I don't really know what to do,
When the weight of the world comes
    between me and you.

We're like the moon chasing the sun,
Somehow we've become intimate strangers.

And as the stars fade in the light,
We both know it ain't right to be alone every night
Like intimate strangers.

Why don't you quit at the diner,
We can make it on just my pay.
I'd rather give it a try and barely get by
    than keep living life this way.

Like the moon chasing the sun,
Until somehow we've become intimate strangers.
And as the stars fade in the light,
We both know it ain't right to be alone every night,
Like intimate strangers.

Copyright 2003, Aaron Cheney

Here's the second set:

The seeds lay cast on stony ground
In ragged rows of red and brown.
And yet he knew the field was good,
Despite the stones he understood,
And let the seeds fall where they would.

He stayed to work the empty field
And in those days the clay did yield.
Just blood and tears and weathered hands
And whisperings of barren land,
A tired but unbroken man.

Like tides the seasons came and went,
The years in fruitless labor spent.
While sickles languished in the dust,
In somber hues of cankered rust
As every tool unneeded must.

But still he toiled with endless passion,
Tilled each row in loving fashion,
And left his lonely benchmark there
Untiring and earnest care,
Until at last an answered prayer.
And now I see the crop he grows,

For golden wheat stands in the rows.
The harvest of a lifetime's plea,
Now finally at the end I see
The seed was him, the field was me.

Copyright 2002, Aaron Cheney

Drum roll please…the first set is the song and the second is the poem. Yeah, I know…I sort of gave it away earlier in the book. Even so, it wasn't difficult to tell them apart. Let's examine why.

First, what is the title of the song? Intimate Strangers, right? You know that because that phrase appeared six times over the course of the song. The rest of the lyrics were important as well, but they were merely orbiting one central idea: the title. Now, what's the title of the poem? Haven't a clue? Could it be "The Farmer"? Nope. How about "Seeds"? Nope. The actual title is "Empty Fields," and that phrase is only mentioned one time. That is the first distinction between the two: songs have a repeating phrase that everything else always leads back to, and poems do not.

There are some exceptions; Poe's The Raven comes to mind. You'll notice however that even though it is the phrase that gets repeated, the title of that poem isn't "Nevermore." This brings us to a second distinction: a person should be able to identify the title of a song after one listening.

Look back for a second at "Empty Fields." You'll see a few phrases like, "the years in fruitless labor spent," and, "as everything unneeded must." Lines like those are another dead giveaway: poem. That isn't how anyone living today talks and it brings us to distinction number three: modern songs don't use arcane language. If you want your song to be successful in today's world, you have to sing it like you say it. Lyrics should be conversational.

Lyrics are to poetry what a fiddle is to a violin—the same instrument played differently. Though closely related in appearance, each manipulates words in unique ways that are only appropriate in the right context. Always work to ensure your lyrics make the title obvious, work back to the chorus, and use conversational speech. No one goes to a hoedown expecting to hear Paganini.

Four Steps to Perfect Lyrics

Lyricists often tend to get ahead of themselves. I know I've done it lots of times: a good idea strikes me and before I know it, I've got a chorus and verse one written and ready to go. And then it happens: suddenly your inspiration hits an iceberg and you're left rowing around with no map or compass like some castaway looking for a place to land. Will verse two ever come to rescue you? It's a sad predicament. That's why I've broken down the process in to four sequential steps.

They are as follows:

1. **Choose a title.**

2. **Lay out your story, situation, or state of mind in plain English, within the framework of a song.**

3. **Write the story as lyrics, using rhyme, meter, and song words.**

4. **Keep re-writing the lyrics until they are perfect.**

Of course, step number four is a killer, but I never said this was going to be easy! Following these steps will help you overcome many of the obstacles songwriters often stumble over. Let's examine them in more detail.

Step 1: The All-Important Title

Every song you write should begin with a title. Starting a set of lyrics without a title is like looking for thumbtacks in a giant home-improvement warehouse store that doesn't have its aisles labeled. The result is a lot of aimless wandering. A title gives direction to, and becomes the returning point for, every other line in your song. I can tell you from sad experience that writing a plot around a great title idea is much easier than trying to find a good title/hook for a story you've already written. Don't let that happen to you!

So, where do good ideas for titles come from? Everywhere! You should always be on the lookout for an interesting turn of phrase, a glib play on words, or a twist on an old cliché. Every magazine, billboard, commercial, or conversation is loaded with possibilities. When something strikes you, write it down in your notebook immediately! What? You don't have it with you? Then write it down on your arm and transfer it to your notebook later (before you take a bath)!

Title possibilities will literally come up anytime or anywhere. Not too long ago I was reading an essay written as a legal briefing. The defending lawyer was trying to establish that his client's accusers weren't as familiar with the situation as they claimed to be. He concluded by sarcastically calling them "intimate strangers." Bam! What a clever contradiction! I wrote those two words down right away, and as you have seen, they sparked the idea for a new song. The lesson? Always be observant, and always have your notebook handy!

Certain phrases make better titles than others. A good title should make someone want to listen to your song. Titles such as, "I Love You," or "What You Mean to Me," are certified yawn-fests. They are tired, overused clichés that have lost their emotional power. Instead, look for something people haven't heard before. Coin a phrase of your own, and make it dynamic, clever, expressive, or active. The following are lists of just a few examples of effective titles:

Use a contradiction in terms or a spin on something familiar: "Eight Days a Week", "If He Were Alive Today (He'd Probably Be Dead)", "A Boy Named Sue".

Try a phrase with a deceptive double meaning: "Muscle of Love" (the heart that is…).

Have all the key words in the title start with the same letter (this is called alliteration): "Winter Wonderland", "Mean Mr. Mustard".

Leave the door "half-open" by using an incomplete phrase that begs further explanation: "Ain't Nothin' Like", "If".

Use a colorful name: "Eleanor Rigby", "Roxanne", "Billy Jean".

Choose an evocative color: "Brown Sugar", "The Green Green Grass of Home", "Blue Skies".

Use an active verb: "Jump", "Beat It".

Encapsulate the entire story in one short phrase: "The Night the Lights Went Out in Georgia".

Once you've decided on a title, don't write yourself into a corner by not checking your title for "rhyme-ability." Spend some time listing rhymes, near rhymes, and related phrases for your title. Make sure you've got plenty of options before committing to it whole-heartedly. Sometimes you'll find you have an interesting phrase that ends with a word that is very difficult to rhyme. Knowing that beforehand gives you the option of re-wording it, inserting it in the middle of a line rather than the end, or just deciding that it's not worth the effort, before you've wasted time building a story around it.

Sometimes as your song develops, you may find that another, better title suggests itself. Don't be afraid to make the switch if your song is improved by doing so. Check your new title idea for rhymes and so forth just as before, and then move forward.

One last note: titles cannot be copyrighted, so don't panic if you find that your song shares a title with someone else's. There have even been instances where two songs with the same title have shared space on the charts at the same time—remember "Jump" by both Van Halen and the Pointer Sisters? Even so, you probably wouldn't want to write a song entitled say, "Eleanor Rigby"…it is too uniquely identified as a Beatles song and too uncommon a phrase to be interpreted any other way.

Step 2: Laying Out the Story

Now that you know the title of your song, it's time to tell your story. Resist the temptation to start writing lines right away, and instead "block out" (example to follow) your story, in plain English, in song form. Taking this extra step helps you know exactly what you are trying to convey in each section of the song before you start struggling with individual words, meter, and rhyme.

The various parts of a song have specific purposes:

<u>The Verse</u>: verses tell the story and move the plot along. Each verse should contain new information yet return to the chorus via the "launch line" or the last line of the verse before the chorus. You should also try to write each verse so that it casts its accompanying chorus in a new light.

<u>The Chorus</u>: the chorus is where the title goes and simply states (and restates) what the song is about. It should be the same or nearly the same every time.

<u>The Bridge</u>: the bridge, or "middle eight," as it's sometimes

called, is used for a plot twist or other new information that takes the story somewhere unexpected. Bridges usually end in one of two ways: they return to the chorus, or precede an instrumental solo. Not every song needs a bridge.

Here's an example of a song idea that's been "blocked out":

Title: "Blacktop Burnout"

<u>Verse 1</u>: Johnny owns a '53 corvette. It's black, and he thinks it can beat any other car it goes up against. He loves to peel out on the pavement. When he does, it's a:

Chorus: Blacktop burnout.

<u>Verse 2</u>: He agrees to race the oldest/toughest guy on the street, who owns a Mustang. The guy's been racing so long he's addicted to it, and he's a:

Chorus: Blacktop burnout.

Bridge: During the race, Johnny loses it in a turn, there's a terrible explosion, and he dies. The fiery wreck is a:

Chorus: Blacktop burnout.

Notice how verse two includes new information and moves the plot along, and how even though verse one and verse two tell different parts of the story, they both lead back to the same thing, the chorus. Also notice how each verse casts its chorus in a different light. In the first chorus, the term "blacktop burnout" refers to Johnny's skid marks. In verse two it refers to the old, burned out racer in the Mustang. The bridge then relates the plot twist, and casts the final chorus in an unexpected light: the "blacktop burnout" is now a fiery wreck. Once you've blocked your song out and you know what each part needs to convey, it's time to write the lyrics!

Step 3: Write the Lyrics

Add it up: the average commercial song has at most thirty lines to introduce the characters, set up the plot, tell the story, and resolve the conflict. That barely leaves room for a guitar solo! Make no mistake—writing lyrics is an art of economy. As John Keats said, "Every line must be loaded with ore." We don't have the room to spread out that a novelist or even a poet does. Every single verse, chorus, line, even word, is precious to a songwriter. Choose them carefully. I'll discuss some ways to do this later in this chapter.

Never assume the listener knows the back-story. You understand the motivations of the characters in your song because you created them. No one else does. You must answer these six basic journalistic questions: who, what, where, when, why, and how.

Remember to unfold the plot by degrees. Don't give everything away in verse 1, or you'll have nothing interesting left to say in verse 2. Likewise, make sure that the second verse isn't just restating the first. Nothing will make a listener's eyes glaze over faster than the dreaded "verse 1 re-hash"! Instead, use it to develop the plot and add new information.

Your song's title should be in the chorus or hook, probably more than once. If they remember nothing else, a person should walk away from your song after one listening knowing what the title is.

Step 4: Rewriting Your Lyrics

Hmm…I think we'll save this step for later. Moving on…

Looking For Rhymes

The concept of the rhyme probably began as a pneumonic device: a way to help people remember things. Rhyming has remained popular ever since, simply because people love novelties in speech. Why just say something, when you can say something glib? It has been a tool in the hands of poets and songwriters for centuries, transforming mere sentences into memorable verses that remain etched in the minds of those who have read or listened to them.

Types of Rhymes

There are many different types of rhymes, with just as many weird sounding names to differentiate them. Rather than embarking upon a grammar lesson, I've chosen instead to call them by their "street names," and focus only on those I've found most helpful and interesting from a songwriter's perspective. They are as follows:

<u>Perfect rhymes</u> are just that, two words whose ending consonants and vowels, sound and are spelled exactly the same: same and blame, brute and absolute.

<u>Imperfect rhymes</u> are similar. The final consonants and vowels sound the same but they are spelled differently. From a songwriter's perspective this difference is moot: cane and plain, become and numb.

<u>False rhymes</u> are those in which the ending vowels of two words sound the same but the consonants do not: done and come, plain and change.

Masculine rhymes are two rhyming words that stress the final syllable: subtract and intact, believe and receive.

Feminine rhymes are two rhyming words whose last syllables are unstressed: number and lumber, mother and brother.

Conglomerate rhymes are created by combining multiple words or fragments of words which are adjacent to one another: compass and bump us, benefit and then if it.

Inside rhymes are rhymes of any type that occur within a line, rather than at the end.

Finding Rhymes

As we discussed before, the first step in songwriting is finding a title and checking it for rhyme-ability. Often you can do this off the top of your head. Begin by listing words that rhyme and seem related to your title. If you get stumped, reach for your rhyming dictionary. Once you have a list, start paring it down to the two or three best rhymes, and get to work. Writing the lines of the lyric can be approached in much the same way. If you have blocked your song out, you already know what you need to say. The challenge is finding the right words to say it. As you search through your rhyming dictionary, you will no doubt come across lots of words that rhyme but have no direct relationship to your story. Don't dismiss them! You can create a relationship via a simile or metaphor and put those words to good use. (More on this later.)

Some songwriters mistakenly think that anything less than a perfect rhyme is a cop-out. Not so. There are only so many perfect rhymes out there, and most of them have already been used to death. (If I have to hear "fire" rhymed with "desire" one more time I'm going to puke!)

False rhymes give you far greater flexibility and make it possible to express yourself in more original ways. They are completely acceptable by today's standards and go hand in hand with creating lyrics that are conversational. Don't ever hesitate to use a false rhyme if it helps you say what you need to say; powerful emotional content always trumps a perfect rhyme.

Sometimes you'll find yourself faced with a line that seems impossible to rhyme. One option is to rearrange your line so that the tough word is in the middle and a different word that is easier to rhyme is at the end. If you simply can't, try looking for false rhymes. This is a situation in which you have to outsmart your rhyming dictionary.

Speech and song are really a series of sustained vowels and transient consonants. Therefore, it is the vowels that are of paramount importance when it comes to rhymes. A good false rhyme must have an ending vowel sound consistent with the word you're trying to rhyme, but the consonant sound can be surprisingly different and still work when sung. For example, imagine you are trying to rhyme the word "rain." You've exhausted every perfect and imperfect rhyme you can think of, and none work. (Thank goodness you didn't use "pain"…that one's been done to death!) Try looking up other words with the long ā sound that end with different consonants, like "ang," "ame," or "ade."

Using Rhymes

Because masculine, feminine, conglomerate, and inside rhymes can also be perfect, imperfect, or false, these types of rhymes are not differentiated by their mechanisms of rhyme, but by their usage. For example, because feminine rhymes leave the final syllables of their words unstressed, you can often "sneak them in" unnoticed after rhyming the middle syllable of the word, like so:

> "But if push comes to shove,
> Find yourself another lover."

That "er" in "lover" just snuck in like someone under the back seat at the drive-in!

It's always best to avoid rhyming a masculine word with a feminine one. It comes off sounding awkward. Arrange the words in your lyrics so that they follow their natural pronunciations.

Conglomerate rhymes are the cleverest type, and the possibilities are virtually limitless. They are especially useful as inside rhymes, but they can work at the end of lines as well. Take this brilliant example from Gaston's song in the Disney movie, Beauty and the Beast, written by Tim Rice: "As a specimen, yes I'm intimidating."

The pairing of "specimen" and "yes I'm in..." is both a conglomerate rhyme and an inside rhyme. Inside rhymes serve two purposes: they make lyrics easier to sing, and they increase the pace of the lyric. If you have a verse section that is starting to feel a little sluggish (often the case in the second verse), sometimes a carefully placed inside rhyme can help to speed the pace up a bit going into the chorus. Be careful not to overuse them, however, or your lyrics may come off sounding too clever. Remember, lyrics should be conversational.

Making Your Lyrics Singable

Unlike poems, lyrics are meant to be sung. Hence, the sound of the words is equally as important as the meaning of the words. For this reason it is vital that you always check your lyrics by singing them. No matter how glib they may be on the page, if they are difficult to sing they are not done yet. Trust your intuition here; if you come across a phrase that just doesn't sound right to you, it's a good bet it needs to be changed.

We have already seen that an inside rhyme can make a lyric more "singable," but it is not the only tool in your woodshed. Here are a few others.

Assonance is the repetition of a vowel sound in a series of words. Basically, it is a string of false rhymes. Assonance makes a lyric easier to sing and speeds up the pace of a line. You've already seen an example of assonance in this line from the song Intimate Strangers:

> "It's lucky for me to be home when
> you leave in the morning."

See how the repeated long "ee" sound gives the line a smooth flow? Compare it to this line:

"It's lucky for me to get back while
you're here in the morning."

Doesn't roll off the tongue nearly as well, does it?

Alliteration, or "head-rhyming" as it is called in some circles, is a series of words with similar sounding beginnings. The most obvious example of alliteration is a tongue twister. Once again, alliteration is a great device to pick up the pace of a lyric and make it easier to sing. To see for yourself how this works, compare these two phrases by reading them aloud:

>Peter Piper picked a peck of pickled peppers.

>Peter the Flutist harvested a bushel of preserved spices.

Prosody is the pattern of stress and intonation in a language, and the practice of arranging words in a lyric according to their natural pronunciation. If that's too much to swallow, just remember this: you have to sing it the way you say it. To quote Mike Meyers, "Don't put the emPHASis on the wrong sylLABle."

When you're writing, you'll often find the word you want to use stresses a syllable that doesn't jive with the meter of the lyric or the melody. Your options are: rearrange the words so that the word you want to use can go elsewhere, or find a different word. Don't become so married to that word that you use it anyway; it will always sound awkward.

Recently I was writing a country song in which I needed to use the word "guitar." Sounds easy enough, right? Problem was, the word "guitar" stresses the second syllable, and it simply wouldn't fit in the lyrics.

I fretted (sorry) over it for weeks, until one day, my wife happened to hear me struggling with the problem. As casually as the office dress code on a Friday, she remarked, "You know, Aaron, real county folks always say the word 'guitar' with the accent on the first syllable. Why don't you just say it the way they do?"

I was stunned. The solution had been so simple, and I had completely missed it. I had forgotten to look deeper. Even worse, I had to share songwriting credit with my wife!

Using A Melody

Writing lyrics to an existing melody is something many songwriters do. (By "existing," I mean a melody from a popular song that somebody else has written.) It helps you to keep the number of syllables consistent through verse and chorus sections, and keeps you from slipping into boring meters that sound too much like poetry.

I have mixed feelings about it. If you intend to write the music yourself, I think it's a really bad idea. You'll have a very hard time writing original music to lyrics that are built around an existing melody. It becomes almost impossible to hear them sung any other way. If writing to a melody really helps you, and you intend to write the music as well, I suggest you compose a quick and original dummy melody that can easily be forgotten once the lyrics are complete. If, on the other hand, someone else will be writing the music, writing lyrics to an existing melody can work, as long as you don't sing them. The minute you do, the jig is up! Either way, the goal is to make sure that corresponding lines in each verse have an equal number of syllables. Not only does this make the song easier to sing, but it makes it more memorable as well.

Making Your Lyrics Interesting

Over-used words and phrases are a barrier to effective communication. Such "dead words" have been abused until they have lost all their emotional power. Don't beat a dead horse with your lyrics. (See…you probably didn't even begin to visualize the cruel beating of an already dead horse; you just skimmed across the words without a second thought because you already knew what they implied.) If you want to write memorable, powerful lyrics, you must go beyond the obvious words and phrases.

Choosing Descriptive Words

When choosing an adjective or adverb, it's easy to reach for one that seems to directly describe the noun or verb it accompanies. I suggest instead that you look for one that does not. This will accomplish a couple of things: it catches the listener off-guard and then makes them think. A large component of successful songwriting is the element of surprise, and unusual descriptive words are a high voltage power line lying across a song's railroad tracks.

Instead of "angry words," try "stormy words" or "poison words." Instead of "ran quickly," try "ran wildly" or "madly." Look deeper for a word that you would never have expected to find and give it a position of importance in your lyrics. Make your listener wonder about how your descriptions relate to the objects and events in your story.

Metaphors and Similes

Metaphors and similes are mainstays of poetry and lyrics.

They are freight trains of descriptive power that work by drawing a comparison between two seemingly unrelated things (like freight trains and descriptions). We were all taught in school that you can tell them apart because a simile employs the words "as a" or "like a" and a metaphor does not.

Examples of similes include:

> Dry as a bone.
> Crazy like a fox.
> Busy as a bee.

Or more interestingly:

> His face was as wrinkled as a trombone player's sleeve.

Examples of metaphors include:

> An ocean of tears.
> Turn the pages of your mind.

Or more interestingly:

> I'm a prisoner in the chamber of your heart.

There is another, more important difference between similes and metaphors that must be taken into consideration when deciding which one might be more effective in your lyrics. Because similes use the qualifiers "like a" or "as a", they are always literally true and leave the phrase feeling resolved. This makes them good for one-time use in lyrics without distracting from a different central idea. Metaphors, on the other hand, are always literally false and may consequently feel unresolved. Often this means they require further explanation. It is not uncommon to see a metaphor used as the central theme for an entire song.

Creating interesting similes and metaphors is something many songwriters struggle with. Once again, it is paramount that you leave your editor's hat in the closet during this process. If yours is on, it's going to tell you that every metaphor you come up with sounds dumb.

Editing hats just don't get—that some of the best metaphors are between the two most disparate things imaginable; like a heart and an anvil, an old man and a question mark, or an improper fraction and an SUV. After all, what on earth could an anvil and a heart have in common? Well…they can both be heavy. An old man and a question mark? They are both hunched over. An improper fraction and an SUV? They are both top-heavy.

The key to creating good similes and metaphors is conveying the unexpected third thing which the first two things have in common. The more unexpected that thing is, the more interesting it will be. Oddly enough, creating metaphors is easiest when you start by knowing the first thing and the third thing, and then look for the second thing. It's like solving a maze…it's often easier starting from the end. Let me show you what I mean.

Let's say you want to create a metaphor for the moon. Your first object becomes the moon. Now, decide which of the moon's qualities it is that you want to describe; maybe its brightness, or its roundness, or its texture, or its revolution around the earth. Whatever the quality is, it will become the third, unexpected element in your metaphor or simile. So let's say it's the roundness that we want to describe. Great!

Now…forget about the moon completely! Put it out of your mind and list only words that describe round. Possibilities might be: a wheel, a hub cap, an old 78 LP, a tennis ball, a pizza, a zero, a donut, a man-hole cover, or the rim of a coffee mug. I'm sure you could go on listing things that are round all day. Once you have your list, pick the one that seems most unusual. Ever hear the following line?

> "When the moon hits your eye like a big pizza-pie, that's amore."

That's how Harry Warren and Jack Brooks chose to describe the moon in their classic song "That's Amore". You could also say:

> The moon rolled across the sky like an old hubcap.

Or:

> I spent the night under heaven's Manhole cover.

Both comparisons are so unusual that they immediately get your attention and make you think about the similarities. Also notice that because, "heaven's man-hole cover" is a metaphor, it begs further explanation, whereas the simile, "the moon rolled across the sky like an old hubcap," is more self-contained.

Creating similes and metaphors is one of my favorite songwriting activities. You can wheel them into your songs like giant Trojan horses and turn them loose. They're much more descriptive than adjectives or adverbs because they don't just tell a listener what to think…they prompt each listener to search their own experiences for a description. Spend some time developing your ability to create unique similes and metaphors; your songs will be better for it!

Opening Lines

Earlier in this section we talked about the precious real estate of words in lyrics. Everyone must count. With no more than thirty lines in your lyrics (usually less), you've got to get to the point quickly, interestingly, and quickly!

The first line is one of tremendous importance. It sets the tone for everything that is to follow. Make sure its language is genre appropriate, and that it's inescapably understandable. Don't leave anyone wondering what in the heck you're talking about!

Next to your title, your opening line is your best chance of getting someone interested enough in your song to stick around for the hook. By the end of line two, you should have established the plot, introduced the characters, and set the mood for the entire song. You should also have established the person and tense of the song. As you write your opening lines, think about how you are addressing the big six journalistic questions: who, what, why, when, where, and how.

The Launch Line

Another line in your song that has great power is the "launch line," the last line of each verse section leading into the chorus. Because each verse should be telling a different part of your story or expressing a new idea, this line serves to bring each verse back around to the central idea of the chorus. It becomes a launching pad into the chorus by explaining how the new material in its verse relates to the main idea of the song.

Tense and Person

As you know, tense refers to the time frame of your song: past, present, or future. Person refers to the point of view. You can write in first person (I, me, and my), second person (you, your, and we), or third person (he, she, and they). First person is far and away the most popular point of view, while "present" is the most popular tense.

Usually a song will occur to you in a certain person or tense. As you block out the story and begin writing the lyrics, take the time to explore the song in different time frames and points of view. Often, you'll find the story or idea works better when expressed in another way. Also, always check that you have made your person and tense consistent throughout the song, from one line to the next. Mistakes often occur between the verse and chorus of the song.

These sentences mix tense:

> She came into the room. She walks over to me.

This sentence mixes person:

> Now she's gone, I miss you so much.

With them right next to each other, it's easy to spot the errors. Separate them by several lines or put them in different song sections, and the inconsistency is harder to spot. A few minutes spent scrutinizing your lyrics can save you from embarrassment later!

Another common mistake many writers make is redundancy. If your lyrics are in first person, make sure you aren't telling other characters in your song things they already know.

Take these lines for example:

> You left me a note
> In the pocket of my coat,
> And these were the words that you wrote:
> You said "I love you,"
> You said "I miss you,"
> And then you sealed it with a kiss.

If someone left you a note in real-life, would you sum up their actions for them? No way! (And I certainly hope you wouldn't write such boring lyrics either! What a yawn-fest!) Instead, tell the story beginning with the moment you found the note, and what you did with it. This may seem nitpicky, but when a listener hears a mistake like this, a little red telephone in the 911 center of their brain starts to ring. They know something's wrong. As a songwriter, it's your job to make sure there is nothing in your song to distract a listener from the story.

Choosing Your Words Carefully

As a lyricist, words are the medium of your trade. We've already discussed many ways in which you can craft interesting, memorable lyrics. Now let's talk about word choice.

<u>Sticking To Your Genre.</u> Perhaps the most important thing when it comes to word choice is selecting words that are appropriate to a song's genre. Nothing gives away an out-of-towner like mispronouncing the name of a city or street, and nothing gives away your ignorance of a genre like using a word that doesn't belong. It shouts to the world, "Hey! I ain't from around here!" For example, using the word "crib" as a euphemism for your home would be entirely inappropriate in

a county song. Also, always be aware of context. The word "hoe" means something very different in a country, rap, or Christmas song.

Words To Avoid. There are thousands and thousands of words out there at your disposal. The more you know, the better off you will be. However, there are certain catagories that for various reasons just don't work well in lyrics. They include:

> Antiquated, arcane, and out-of-use words. Hard-to-pronounce words like quagmire, arcane and antiquated.
>
> Diseases and medical terms (unless they pertain to the heart).
>
> Words with more than three syllables (except words that end with "tion").

Recently I was asked by a fellow songwriter to offer my opinion about a song he had written. He began by giving me the song's title: Wax and Wane. He then went on to explain that the terms "wax" and "wane" refer to the rising and setting of the moon. My immediate response was, 'If you feel like you need to define those words for me, there is no way you should be using them in your lyrics.' Despite some great visual imagery in the song, its entire framework was built upon the crumbling foundation of arcane, out-of-date words.

Hard to pronounce words and words with more than three syllables should be avoided simply because they are hard to sing. Medical and scientific terms are also hard to sing, but more than that, they are often too deep, technical, or downright ghastly to include in a song. Nobody wants to hear about a gastric bypass set to music!

Many songwriters also make the mistake of using too many words. Songs that are overly wordy sound heavy, like too much paint on a wall. Pay particular attention to songs with a fast tempo. It doesn't take much verbiage before they begin to sound crowded. When in doubt, err on the side of simplicity and minimalism. Make your songs easy for a listener to follow and understand (and sing along to).

Another pitfall to avoid is talking directly to the listener—it almost never works, particularly as a moral conclusion in the last verse of a song. Any song whose last verse starts with words like, "So if you don't want this to happen to you…" is about to fall flatter than week-old root beer. Lyrics like those just come off preachy and contrived. If you have a point you want to make, it's much more effective to make it via a poignant story, and let the listener draw their own conclusions, than to tell them what to think.

The Balancing Act

As a wordsmith honing one's craft, it's often tempting to stretch for something glib, clever, or deep. While very gratifying for you as a writer, such things often leave listeners uninterested. People these days are busy, and most simply don't feel like delving into the hidden subtleties of a flowery, poetic lyric. In the 30's and 40's, glib wordplay was all the rage and songwriter's like Cole Porter were masters at manipulating the English language. Modern lyrics, with the exception of show-tunes, are conversational. It's sad but true. You must sing it like you say it.

Make your songs fascinating. Discover those brilliant metaphors that give your songs dimension and emotional content. Look for clever inside rhymes and alliterations to make your songs more singable. But above all, use such things in moderation! Strike a balance between clever and emotional/conversational, and when forced to choose, err on the side of emotional/conversational. Use your intuition to determine when you've tipped the scales too far...that little voice inside your head is usually right.

At some point in your life, I'm sure you've heard someone say something to the effect of, "There are no words to describe how I feel," or "Words fail me." What a load of hooey! I have more confidence in words than that, and as a songwriter so should you! Words are powerful. Anyone that believes "words are not enough," has never heard them set to music. Your challenge as a songwriter is to find those unique things from your own experience and use them in your songs as a gateway to experiences we all share.

Don't be afraid to express yourself in ways that make you vulnerable. Powerful emotional songs are never guarded. Love, passion, anger, rage, confusion, sorrow, pain, anguish, joy…these are the stuff of truly great songs.

I sincerely believe that lyrics and music are one of man's highest forms of expression. Powerful lyrics aren't an accident. They happen through consistent effort and experience. I promise you that if you apply the techniques we've discussed here, the quality (and quantity) of your lyrics will improve.

Chapter Four
Crafting Great Music

Writing Music Isn't Just For Musicians

As we discussed earlier, writing music does not require a deep knowledge of music theory or even the ability to play a musical instrument. If you can hear the music in your head and communicate it to another musician, you can write music. Find a friend that plays guitar or piano and offer to pay them for their time. Sing your melodies to them and have them transcribe them for you. Once you've given them your melody, most musicians will be able to suggest chords to accompany it. Have them try a variety of chords behind your melody until you discover what works best. You'll be surprised how effective and rewarding this approach can be. That is not to say that learning music theory or how to play an instrument won't make you a better songwriter. The more you know, the better and more varied your songs will be. Just as increasing your vocabulary makes you a more well-rounded lyricist, knowing the mechanisms of music will give you a greater palette of musical choices.

This section does not focus on music theory. Rather, it deals specifically with song construction. Because it is difficult at times to talk about one without the other, non-musicians may come across some references to theory with which they are unfamiliar. Take some time to wrap your brain around these relatively simple concepts…you'll be glad you did.

The Components of a Song

Music is composed of three things: melody, harmony, and rhythm. Melody is the part of the song you sing. It gives the song musical direction. The harmony is all the other notes surrounding the melody. They create musical dimension and depth. Rhythm is the framework of time into which the melody and harmony are fit. An arrangement of these three building blocks is a song.

Though not required, songwriters generally create songs by organizing the elements of melody, harmony, and rhythm into repeating patterns. This makes them more pleasing and memorable. These repeating patterns are known as a song's verse and chorus. To add variety, songwriters may also use non-repeating sections at various places within a song. These include bridges, intros, outros, and solos.

The Repeating Parts

The verse and chorus sections are the backbone of a song. We've already discussed their purposes from a lyrical point of view. Their purposes from a musical point of view are closely related. The melody during a verse is often busy and the accompaniment is more subdued. Here, listeners are trying to follow the story. Don't distract them! The vocals are generally in a lower range, making it easier for a singer to enunciate and speak clearly.

During the chorus, the melody becomes simpler. Meanwhile, the accompaniment gets more complex for maximum dramatic impact. The chorus is also generally sung in a higher register than the rest of the song. The chorus is a restatement of the song's theme, and the music should help drive that idea home.

The Non-Repeating Parts

An intro begins a song and could almost be considered a

repeating part. Its primary function is to set the tone for the song and usher in the first verse, but often its musical theme is identical to that of the chorus.

We already know that the bridge is the place for a plot twist. Similarly, it is also a good place to introduce new chords or musical themes. Placing them here accentuates the fact that there is something new going on and reminds the listener to pay attention.

Outros are either a musical tag that ends the song, or in this era of modern technology, a volume fade. In the later case, the fade usually occurs while the musicians vamp on the chorus. In songs that spotlight a musical soloist, the fade can also occur over an extended solo.

Instrumental solos in most pop songs should be kept short, especially if you intend to market the song to other artists. Don't let them run longer than eight measures at most. Obviously, if the intent of your song is to spotlight a soloist, you should include extended solos.

All the Parts Together

Songwriters often combine their verses, choruses, and other song sections in similar orders. These orders are called song forms. Different song forms lend themselves to different types of songs or genres. Listed below are the most common song forms along with an example or two of each:

A = One section that does not repeat; "Frère Jacques", and "The Wreck of the Edmond Fitzgerald", by Gordon Lightfoot. This form usually has the feel of an old English air.

AA = Two sections that repeat the same melody using different lyrics; "This Land is Your Land" by Woodie Guthrie and "Skip to my Lou".

AAA = Three sections that share the same melody with different lyrics; "Annie's Song", by John Denver. Many traditional blues songs also use this form, and the last line of each section is usually the title hook.

AABA = Three sections that all share the same melody with a bridge to provide a break; "Heavy Cloud No Rain", by Sting.

ABAB = Verse, chorus, verse, chorus; "Wind Beneath My Wings", by Henley and Silbar.

ABABCB = Verse, chorus, verse, chorus, bridge, chorus; "Nothing's Gonna Stop Us Now", by Warren and Hammond; "That's the Way It Is", by Martin, Lundin, and Carlsson.

In modern, popular music, the ABAB or ABABCB forms are the most popular. The verse sections in these forms may also contain a "ramp" or "pre-chorus" section that transitions into the chorus. Either form may also incorporate a third verse. In ABABCB form, it usually occurs after the bridge or "C" section. If you choose to add a third verse, make sure it is adding new information that further develops the story and doesn't make the song seem longish.

Some songwriters feel that using standard song forms is giving in to commercialism. While it is true that many great songs eschew standard song form, it also true that most successful songs adhere to them. As stated at the beginning of this book, the purpose of your song dictates the kind of song you should write. If you prefer to write songs outside the conventions of song form because you will be performing them yourself or for art's sake, by all means do it! If, on the other hand, commercial success as a songwriter is your goal, you must stick to standard song form to give yourself any reasonable chance.

Conventional song forms are not a limitation. Any gifted songwriter can be just as creative within their framework as without. Spend some time learning to understand the various forms and how they work. Once you're armed with this understanding, your gut will tell you when it's appropriate to take that left turn instead of the normal right!

The Melody

As we have already discussed, the melody is the part of the song that you sing. This places it at the top of the heap in order of importance. As a songwriter, you want your listeners to walk away humming the tune after one listening. It follows, that your job is to write a melody that is both memorable and singable.

Finding A Melody

The first question is: where do melodies come from? Often a melodic idea will suggest itself the minute you come across a title idea. The prosody and subject matter instantly scream, "Sing me this way!" Hand-held memo recorders are great for quickly documenting your melody in those fleeting first moments. Other possible sources for melody ideas include:

- chord progressions
- a riff or instrumental line
- other lyrics or hooks besides the title
- the rhythm
- the tone of the lyrics, a mood, or a visual image

Creating a melody that follows a pre-determined chord

progression (a pleasing sequence of chords) is a tried-and-true method, especially for guitarists, and has been the genesis for thousands of great songs. It's also a trap that can make for boring songs. If you are a guitar player who struggles with melodic originality, practice writing lyrics a cappella (with your voice only).

Other songwriters can benefit from this technique too. It frees you from old instrumental habits and musical patterns and lets your melodic ideas flow more freely. Work out the accompaniment only after the melody is clearly established.

Besides strumming chord progressions, guitarists also tend to write riff-based songs. A riff—short for refrain—is a repeating instrumental line that usually begins a song and then forms part of the chorus. It is an instrumental hook. Think of the opening guitar parts for "Day Tripper", by the Beatles, or "Cat Scratch Fever", by Ted Nugent here! When writing a melody over a riff, try to avoid letting it follow the same rhythm or sequence of notes. It should become its own line.

Sometimes a mood or visual image can influence how you write. If you are writing a melody to lyrics about the death of a loved one, chances are, you would write it differently than another melody about a hottie at the local dance hall. Look for notes that portray the appropriate mood, even without the lyrics. Minor scales are generally sad or unsettled, while major scales are neutral or happy.

Generally speaking, a good melody:

- has movement
- is easy to sing
- resolves
- fits the mood of the lyrics
- lends itself to varied arrangements

Ask ten songwriters what a good melody is, and you will likely get back twenty different answers and a fistfight. Most will agree, however, that melody writing is one of the most difficult aspects of songwriting. The melody is the wellspring of the entire song. Just as with lyrics, your first impulse with a melody may not always be the best, and re-writes will be necessary. The following sections describe additional things to keep in mind as you write and re-write your melody.

Making It Memorable and Interesting

In order for a listener to sing your melody, they first must remember your melody. Music has a profound effect on the human mind that goes far beyond the scope of this book.

Suffice it to say that it is an interesting phenomenon that most people can remember a melody without the lyrics, but not vice versa. That does not mean that all melodies are equally memorable. Certain techniques can make a melody stand out.

A melody can be broken down into phrases, and those phrases can be further broken down into motifs. A motif can be as small as two notes. Keeping your phrases short makes them more memorable. As an example let's examine this line from the Beatle's song, "Get Back":

"Get back…get back…get back
to where you once belonged."

In this phrase, the notes to the words "get back" are the first motif. The second motif contains identical notes and lyrics. The notes that accompany the words, "Get back to where you once belonged," are the motif that completes the phrase. See how easy it is to remember? It's broken down into two catchy, two-note motifs that cling to the brain like superglue. They are "mini-hooks" that interest and engage the listener.

The third and final motif begins with the exact same notes as the first two before adding the remaining notes that resolve the phrase. It should also be noted that between each "get back" the song is punctuated with a musical hook played by the guitar and drums. It's such an integral part of the song that it's almost impossible to imagine the song without it! The Beatles were indeed masters at loading their songs with hooks!

You should also strive to write melodies that make it obvious where the title goes even without the lyrics present. Try altering the range of the melody during the title phrase. Inserting a dramatic pause directly before or after the title is also very effective. You can also alter the rhythm of the title phrase to set it apart from the rest of the melody.

By following clues contained in the lyrics, you can make your melody unique. For example, if the lyric contains the words "higher and higher," you might consider writing a melody that does just that, ascending in pitch with each successive word. In the Garth Brooks' hit, "I've Got Friends in Low Places", the word "low" is the lowest note in the line. Of course, in the song, "Ring of Fire", Johnny Cash sings the words, "I went down, down, down," but the notes go up, up, up. Lesson: don't rewrite a great melody just to appease a few words in a lyric.

Vary the rhythmic pulse of the melody to differentiate the verse, chorus, and bridge. The songs "Fly Away", by Lenny

Kravitz, and "Ain't Talkin' 'Bout Love", by Van Halen, are both built on a chord progression that does not change during the entire course of the song. To maintain interest in such songs, it is vital that the rhythm of the melody change from verse to chorus.

As your write, be aware that certain scales or melodic rhythms will immediately invoke a particular mood or genre. A harmonic minor scale will always create an exotic, restless mood. A blues scale will likewise identify your song as a blues song. Patriotic, cartoon, and "school spirit" songs also hinge around particular rhythms and scales in their melodies. Make sure to avoid them (unless that is your intent).

Making Your Melody Singable

This is another area where the purpose of your songs dictates the kind of song you should write. If you intend to perform it yourself, you can write it to suit your own particular singing style. If, on the other hand, you hope to have others perform it, you need to write in a style more generally singable. In both cases you also need to bear your audience in mind. If they can sing it themselves, they are more apt to enjoy and remember it.

In general, melodies should be linear. In other words, they should ascend and descend on adjacent notes in a given scale. Musically speaking, an interval is the distance between two notes in a scale. Big intervals are tough for most people to sing. Classic examples of songs with difficult interval jumps are "The Christmas Song", by Mel Torme, and "Somewhere Over the Rainbow", by Arlen and Harburg, whose opening two notes are an entire octave apart. "Twinkle Twinkle Little Star" begins with a more manageable jump of only a fifth, but even that is a stretch for most people.

Your songs should be in a key that is easy for most people to sing in. Additionally, try to keep the melody within a reasonable range; don't go too high or too low. Doing so will make your melody accessible to a wider range of singers. Who hasn't bonked while singing, "and the rockets' red glare" from "The Star Spangled Banner"? I love the U.S. national anthem, but Francis Scott Key broke just about every songwriting rule in the book on that one!

Finally, keep the sound of the lyrics in mind as you craft the melody. Certain sounds are easier to sing in certain ranges than others. For example, the sounds "oh" as in "go," "eh" as in "said" and "ah" as in "father" are easy to sing in a very high range. Conversely, the sounds "ee" as in "see" and "oo" as in "cool" are very difficult. Make it easy for the singer by placing open vowels sounds on difficult high notes and closed vowel sounds on lower notes where they are not a struggle.

From a commercial point of view, writing a melody that is widely singable makes your song marketable to a wider range of singers. It also gives an audience the chance to sing along and connect with the artist and the song.

Fishing for Hooks

At their most basic (and boring), hooks are just specific musical or lyrical phrases that recur enough times in a song to be remembered. For example, the title of a song is usually a hook. However, good hooks are something more. Good hooks are like a musical ambush. They catch a listener by surprise, grab their attention, and engage them in the song. They are memorable both lyrically and musically.

Hooks do not live on their own. They exist in a strange symbiotic relationship with the other components of a song. They are almost always found clinging to a chorus, but often can turn up in verses, bridges, and just about any other part of a song. The more a songwriter can get in one song the better. In fact, a really great song has more hooks than the local fishing hole on opening day!

As a songwriter you can purposefully write hooks, and just like anything else, your ability to write powerful hooks increases the more you practice. A hook can be as simple as a repeated lyric or phrase. A skilled songwriter can craft a hook that is more memorable and appealing than that by applying different techniques to make it stand out. Some ways to do this are with a dramatic pause, a rhythmic twist, or a sudden "surprise" note that comes out of the blue.

As we just discussed, melodies are usually best kept linear (without too many big interval skips) because that makes it easier for most people to sing. However, linear melodies are often emotionally neutral. When you arrive at a point in the lyrics where you want to really provoke a powerful emotion, throw in a big interval jump. Works every time.

Let's go back for a second to "The Christmas Song" and "Somewhere Over the Rainbow". The people who wrote those songs knew that using a large interval skip on the first two notes of the melody would make it difficult to sing. They chose to use them anyway, and to great effect! They create an immediate sense of drama and powerful emotional content. From the first two notes, the listener is engaged, and anything that engages a listener is a hook!

Remember:

> linear = emotionally neutral
> big intervals = emotionally powerful

Good hooks should also take a listener by surprise. If you haven't caught their interest, you still have work to do. Take the following four-line chorus for example. I've only revealed the first three lines. Can you guess what the fourth line will be?

> I love you.
> I love you.
> I love you…

What's coming next? Yep, you guessed it: "I love you." Yawn. The only hook here is the Vaudeville hook coming out from behind the curtain to drag those crappy lyrics off the stage! In order to engage your listener you must surprise them! Let's try the same chorus again with a slight change:

> I love you.
> I love you.
> I love you.
> 'Cause I'm stupid.

See how much more engaging that chorus is once it contains a surprise? Musical hooks can be surprising as well. Set the listener up with three similar melody lines, use the fourth line to deliver a rhythmical curve, a surprise note, or a big interval jump, and then resolve it.

Arranging Your Tune

Arranging is the process of deciding which notes, instruments, and rhythms will accompany your melody. This is where the remaining two elements of music, namely harmony and rhythm, come in.

Usually a melody will suggest which chords might accompany it, but often you can manipulate or substitute the "obvious" chords for other, more interesting ones. If you have a repeating series of notes in your melody, you can make them sound new by playing a different chord under them each time through.

Don't get too crazy though…complex chord changes can be hard to grasp for the average listener. Genres that make use of these kinds of changes, such as jazz and fusion, are usually aimed at a "musically educated" audience.

The Almighty I, IV, V

Without straying too deep into music theory, let's take a second and talk about what is far and away the most common chord progression in modern popular music: the I, IV, V. (Musicians refer to this as a "one, four, five".) Don't let the Roman numerals intimidate you; the concept is actually very simple. If you are harmonizing in the key of C, the C major triad becomes the "I," or "one." For guitar players, this means your C chord is your "one." The "one" is the chord that resolves your song. It's the home chord. To find the IV and the V, simply number each successive note in the key of C, like so:

1	2	3	4	5	6	7
I	II	III	IV	V	VI	VII
C	D	E	F	G	A	B

(Notes in the key of C)

The F chord then becomes the IV, or "four," and the G chord becomes the V, or "five." So a I, IV, V (or "one, four, five") in the key of C would be a chord progression built upon the C, F, and G chords. You don't have to play country music very long before you come across about a zillion songs that use only those three chords.

Just to make sure we've got it, let try it again in the key of E:

1	2	3	4	5	6	7
I	II	III	IV	V	VI	VII
E	F#	G#	A	B	C#	D#

(Notes in the key of E)

Using the chart above it's easy to see that a I, IV, V in the key of E is: E, A, B. You don't have to play rock or blues music very long before you come across about a zillion songs that use only those three chords.

Take some time to play through I, IV, V's in various keys and become familiar with the sound. As you listen to music, try to recognize which songs use this chord progression. It will turn up in all kinds of songs from "Old MacDonald had a Farm" to "Come Together", by the Beatles or "Pride and Joy", by Stevie Ray Vaughan. You will be amazed by the amount and variety of songs that are built upon this simple principle. All this in no way implies that you should avoid using other chords in your songs. A deeper knowledge of music theory will only strengthen your skill as a songwriter, giving you more choices and means of adding color and dimension to your songs.

Chord progression can also be either major or minor. Remember: generally major keys are happy or neutral and minor keys are brooding. Use the subject matter of your lyrics as a litmus test when deciding which to use for a given song.

Give Me A Beat

While melody and harmony provide musical direction and depth, it's a song's rhythmic structure that holds everything together and ties it most strongly to a particular genre. So strongly, in fact, that it is entirely possible to transform a song's genre by altering only its rhythm. For example, contrast John Denver's version of his well-known song "Take Me Home, Country Roads", with its classic folk beat, to the Toots & the Maytals recording. In their version, the melody and chords remain unchanged, but by giving the rhythm a chopping backbeat, it takes on all the characteristics of classic reggae.

Modern pop music is almost exclusively written in 4/4 time or one of its triplet variations, such as 12/8. Occasionally a song in 3/4, such as "I'm With You", by Avril Levine and The Matrix, will find its way to the charts, but that is rare. More complex time signatures normally fall within the realm of jazz or "musician's music."

Within 4/4 time, genres are differentiated by the way they accent the various downbeats and upbeats in a measure. Rock and roll, for example, relies on a heavy backbeat that emphasizes beats 2 and 4. Country music, on the other hand, emphasizes beats 1 and 3. Staccato (or short and sharp) upbeat accents give styles like soul, funk, and reggae their recognizable sounds. Latin music is a world unto itself and contains a myriad of unique and interesting flavors, all accenting different parts of a measure: meringue, samba, flamenco, and bossa nova, just to name a few. Artists like Paul Simon have infused such rhythms into American pop music with intriguing results.

Song Development

The parts of a song are inextricably linked. You might have the best, most memorable chorus in the world, but without the verses setting it up properly it won't work. Every part of a song depends on every other part of the song to do its job. A song just isn't finished until every part is important and fulfilling its function.

As you listen to your song, you may begin to have a sense that your second verse is dragging. You've already heard the melody and chords once before. Hopefully you've arranged your lyrics properly and verse two is telling a new part of the story. There are musical things you can do to maintain a listener's interest as well. Bring in a new instrument or musical line: even something as simple as a tambourine in the second verse can wake a listener up and make them think, "Hey! I haven't heard this before!"

Even if your accompaniment is a single instrument, you can vary the part it plays somewhat between verses. Usually the most appropriate thing to do is have its part become more complex as the song goes on, building tension until the final chorus.

Other times you will find yourself stuck in a song, trying desperately to add elements that will make it work. As you arrange your tune, keep in mind that often what makes a song work is not what you put in, but what you leave out. Learn to use space in your songs. Let them breathe. Sting is a master at minimalist arranging, and his Police song, "Walking on the Moon", is a beautiful example. There's almost enough space in that song for a whole 'nother song!

Breaking the Rules

Wow...it sounds so dangerous! Many budding songwriters just can't resist the allure of living on the wild side—but breaking the rules should be a product of understanding, not inexperience. Make sure that any time you break the rules, you do so only because it works for the song.

Just for fun, I've listed a few better-known rule breaking songs below. Listen to them and figure out why they still work despite their "flaws."

"Eleanor Rigby", by Lennon/McCartney, no choruses. It starts with a bridge and then alternates between bridges and verses for the rest of the song.

"Annie's Song", by John Denver, an "A" song form with no verses or chorus. The title isn't even found anywhere in the song. Heck, it doesn't even rhyme!

"Every Breath You Take", by Sting, no verses. It starts with the chorus, and then goes to a bridge section. Halfway through the song there's a second, different bridge section!

"The Wreck of the Edmond Fitzgerald", by Gordon Lightfoot, no verses or choruses…just a simple "A" form song with the feel of an old English folk tune or Scottish air.

"Lovesick Blues", by Hank Williams, switches between first and third person.

Ninety-nine point nine percent of the time, "rule-breakers" are written by the same artists who perform them. That is the case with each of the songs above. None of them would have been very likely to get picked up by another artist. Even so, each artist broke the rules in a brilliant way and has proven their song to be a great one.

If practiced, the techniques we've discussed in this section will make your songs more singable and memorable. Remember that just as your first draft of lyrics is rarely your best, your first melodic instincts may also need to be re-written. Don't settle until your music is perfect.

Chapter Five
You've Got A Song

Rewriting

The first draft of a song is almost never the best draft. A hit song requires careful crafting through a process of alternately evaluating and reworking it (as many times as it takes) until it is perfect.

During this process, it can be helpful to seek the opinions of other songwriters and even industry professionals to help you hammer out the fine points. I always liken the process to a rough piece of granite that has fallen into a river. It begins jagged, but over time the river chips a point off here, and smooths an edge there, and eventually the stone is polished.

Evaluating Your Song

One of the best ways to evaluate your new masterpiece is to perform it (or have it performed by someone else.) You can find "open mic" nights just about anywhere. They are casual performances usually held on Sunday or Monday nights at local clubs or halls. They offer budding songwriters a chance to perform their tunes, listen to what other songwriters are doing, and rub shoulders with fellow musicians. Call around and find the time and location of one near you.

Your first open-mic can be a little scary. Show up early enough that you have time to get signed up and "acclimate" yourself to the new surroundings. Performing your song is a great way to test the lyrics for "singability" and learn how audiences respond to what you've done. If you can't sing or play, find someone who can. Even if you can play, you might consider having someone else perform your song for you. Doing so offers some delicious advantages: you get to hear the song from a consumer's point of view, plus…you get to sit anonymously in the audience and judge honest reactions.

If you can't find an open mic night, take advantage of get-togethers with your friends and family and perform for them. Sing your song to yourself if that's your only option. In order to work the kinks out of your song you've got to hear it.

Another option is to record your song and solicit the opinions of other songwriters. There are many BBS and Internet radio services where songwriters routinely post songs, critique each other's work, and collaborate.

If you own a computer and basic recording software, it's very simple to record your song, save it as an mp3, and upload it to the Internet. You can literally receive opinions from people all over the world.

Seeking Professional Help

There are many professional song-help services that will review your songs and give you constructive feedback for a fee. If you feel your songs are nearing a professional level, opinions like this can be worth the money. Be prepared to be thick-skinned. These are industry professionals that see hundreds of good songs every month. They will be absolutely honest in appraising your song, whether you like their opinion or not!

You can also enter your song in a contest. Song contests can be found in magazines, books, and on the Internet. Usually the entry fee is $10 to $30 dollars. The quality of such contests can vary widely. In some, the only way you ever even know you entered is because they cash your check! Better ones are those that include a free magazine subscription or some other benefit to all who enter. The best are those that offer to give you feedback on your entry. Having an insider listen to your song and offer advice is well worth the entry fee alone.

Doing the Rewrites

Once you've spent some time evaluating your song, it's time to get back to work. Let's get this out in the open right now: everybody hates rewrites…amateur and pro alike! It's akin to finishing construction on a house, only to be told that all the plumbing must be redone. Suddenly you're faced with having to tear out trim and knock down drywall just to get to the pipes. It stinks. The good news is, for those who press on there is a better song just up ahead.

If you've been performing or listening to your song arranged a certain way for a while, it may become difficult for you to hear it any other way. If you find this is the case, try this: rewrite Twinkle Twinkle Little Star, Mary Had a Little Lamb, or Happy Birthday. Changing the melody to a song you've always considered unalterable is a good ice breaker. It also lets your mind get started without the pressure of working on something that "really matters."

We've already talked about your creative hat and your editing hat, and how they don't work together well. This is your editing hat's chance to shine, but there's also a third hat that people sometimes wear during the re-writing process. It's called the "ego hat," and it doesn't play well with the editing hat at all. When your editing hat (or a co-writer) says, "this needs to be fixed because it isn't working," your ego hat will immediately jump in with, "What are you talking about? I worked on that for hours and it's perfect!" It's time to take off the ego hat and throw it in the closet; and trust me…it won't go without a fight. Don't give in. Your ego hat doesn't care about your song; all it cares about is itself. If you acquiesce, your song will suffer.

Make sure to distance yourself from your song a little so that you can approach it objectively. Give it a day, a week, or a month. In some cases a song may sit for even longer, and that's alright too. I've had several instances where I've had to set aside a song for much longer than that. After working on it for weeks and getting nowhere, I made the decision to shelve it and move on.

Getting back to a song as long as two years later, I was able to complete it in short order. Why? Somewhere in that space of time I found the input, influence, inspiration, life experience, or whatever you want to call it, that the song needed. I could have worked feverishly day and night the previous years and never finished the song because I didn't have the raw materials I needed then.

Don't be in a hurry, and trust your intuition to know when it's perfect. Many times there will be one line that just bugs you every time you hear it. That's your intuition trying to tell you that, that line needs more work. Don't ignore it. If your song gets left that way, it will haunt you every time you hear it for the rest of your life. A bad song cannot be fixed later or "in the mix," and it's important to make sure everything is just right.

All commercial songs have four things in common:

- they are filled with great hook
- they are simple
- they are memorable
- they have wide appeal

As you refine your song, look for these hallmarks, especially if your aim is to market your songwriting. Even if you intend to perform you own songs and aren't interested in being "commercial", strive to refine them to a point where all the elements of your song are doing their part and not a single note or lyric seems out of place or odd. Rewriting is both the most difficult and most rewarding part of the songwriting process. It is the refiner's fire. Don't sell your songs short by accepting the first draft.

Collaboration

Nothing epitomizes the "art of compromise" like two songwriters working together. At its best, you have a pairing whose total is greater than the sum of the parts. Legendary songwriting teams like Lennon and McCartney have written songs that will outlive them.

Opportunities to find a songwriting partner abound. In addition to places like open-mic nights, many cities have songwriters' associations. These are a wonderful resource. They almost always provide a supportive, creative atmosphere where tunesmiths of all experience levels work to help each other improve their craft. Many are free, while some charge a modest yearly fee to cover expenses.

Many community and local colleges also offer continuing education classes on songwriting. These may be conducted either in a weekly or bi-weekly class or as a one-day workshop. Fees usually run about $60. Keep your eyes peeled for other songwriters who write in similar genres or who share common musical interests.

Collaboration can be a struggle when each partner has a different vision of where a song should go. This is another time when your ego hat should be in the closet. It's OK to argue your position passionately when you feel strongly about a certain melody or arrangement. Just make sure it's the song that you're protecting and not your ego hat.

If worse comes to worst, don't be afraid to walk away from a collaboration that is going nowhere. Don't jeopardize your creativity by staying in a dead-end partnership out of sheer loyalty. Have the courage to move on and the faith that something better will present itself.

Being Critical of Your Criticism

Once you begin playing your songs for others you will start to receive opinions and criticism. Some of it will be kind, some will be scathing. The vast majority of it will be worthless. It's important for a songwriter to be able to differentiate between helpful, productive criticism and all the rest. What other people think is only valuable if they're the right kind of critic.

Cheerleaders

Cheerleading critics include family and friends trying to be supportive. For this reason they tell you everything you do is wonderful. While it's important to have them in your corner cheering you on, you must remember that their advice and opinions do not come from an extensive musical background or experience in the music industry. Accept their praise for what it is and bask in the glow of your greatest fans, but look elsewhere for valuable criticism.

Ignoramuses

Like cheerleaders, ignorant critics don't have any real experience to draw from…but they think they do. They are also well-meaning people, but their advice is often along the lines of, "That's a great song…now what you need to do is contact the DJ down at KSUX and get that on the radio," or "I can hear Alan Jackson singing that song. You need to get a copy to him." Even worse is this sage advice: "That's a great song. You should do something with it!"

Anyone with ten minutes of experience in the music industry knows things are rarely that simple. Again, accept their praise but look elsewhere for guidance.

Jerks

These are people who, for whatever reason, have built their identity around being bullies. They thrive on being in control and will squash others whenever the opportunity presents itself. Here's a story to illustrate what I mean.

Some time ago I inquired about joining a songwriters' association in my area. I sent them a letter (all I had was an address) and got a packet a few days later from the fellow that chaired the association. It requested three lyric sheets and an SASE. I sent them off immediately, along with a cover letter. In my haste, however, I forgot to enclose the SASE.

About a week later, I received a reply. This person had enclosed another copy of the instruction sheet with the words, "Please send a SASE," double underlined, and the words, "When all else fails, try following instructions," written in fat black marker in the margin. He also included my cover letter with this note on it (this time in red marker): "Where's the SASE that was specifically requested in the letter?" He even went so far as to return my original mailing envelope on which I had mistakenly abbreviated the word association as "ass." Written next to it (again in red marker) were these words: "An ass is a donkey, or someone who acts like one. The abbreviation for association is assn."

I felt completely humiliated. This person was willing to buy an envelope and a stamp out of his own pocket to ridicule and berate me, but not to return my lyric sheets or send me whatever info the SASE was supposedly intended for. Frankly, the fact that he returned everything I had sent, even down to the envelope I mailed them in, but not my lyric sheets, had me wondering what his motivations might be.

No point in engaging the jerk, I decided. I took the high road and sent him a second letter (this time with an SASE and the word "association" properly abbreviated!) requesting that he simply use the envelope to return my lyric sheets. A few days later I received my SASE back with a single note inside (red Sharpie, for those keeping track) that read, "You and I seem to be having trouble communicating. I asked for three lyric sheets and an SASE!! Try again."

In the heat of the moment, I found his number on the instruction sheet and phoned him…(always a mistake). The conversation did not go well and accomplished nothing. It's tough to maintain your ambition when you come across someone like this. Your ego takes a beating, especially when the person in question is pouncing on a mistake you made like a hyena on a wounded zebra. Work through it with the understanding that this is only one miserable person. Put your shoulder back to the wheel and forge ahead with dogged determination. If you don't feel like writing or promoting your songs anymore, keep writing and promoting until you do.

I never received my lyric sheets back. Fortunately for me, the songs I sent had all been copyrighted. The best news is that one of them, Intimate Strangers, has gone on to become an award-winning song. Had I floundered in my woes and let one unhappy person sway me from my goal I would have missed the wonderful high point that came when one of my songs succeeded.

A Mentor

Feedback from an informed, experienced songwriter is the most valuable kind of criticism. Every artist needs a critic like this; someone with experience and a discerning ear whose opinion they can trust. Someone who cannot only tell you what you've done wrong, but what to work on and how to fix it. Having someone like this in your corner is a rare blessing and can be vital to your success.

Network. Go to open mic nights and association meetings. Once you've discovered this person, stay close to them and let them know you value their opinion.

The Final Critic

These are your songs. You have the final say. Be honest about them, trust you own intuition, and write every song as if it were the most important one of your career. At the same time, don't be too hard on yourself. Give yourself the opportunity to write better songs in the future by learning from the songs you are writing today and moving on.

Protecting Your Songs

By law, your song is copyrighted the moment you have it recorded on some fixed medium, such as a cassette, CD, or piece of sheet music. Protecting your copyright, however, requires that you have it registered with the U.S. Copyright Office. Doing so is easy and relatively cheap. First, you need to get your hands on the paperwork. You can download the forms you need here:

http://www.copyright.gov/forms/

It is important that you fill out the correct form for the type of copyright you are registering. In general, songwriters are most concerned with form PA. It protects the song itself. If you have recorded the song and wish to protect your actual audio recording from being broadcast, sampled, or used as a component in someone else's work, you should use form RA. The fee is $30 per form, but you are allowed to group songs together as a "collection." At the end of every year, I generally burn a CD of all the songs I've written during that time and call it something like, "The Aaron Cheney 2012 Collection." That way I'm able to secure a copyright on all of them, but I only pay the fee once.

Once you've completed the form, enclose it with a check and good quality copies of your songs, and mail them to the Copyright Office via Certified Mail. Make sure to request a return receipt. I advise this because even though your copyright is officially registered the day they receive your paperwork, it sometimes takes a whopping eight or nine months before you get it back. That extra fifty cents at the Post Office buys me a year's worth of reassurance that they actually have my songs and are processing my copyright!

A long standing myth in the world of music is that you can establish a copyright date by mailing yourself a copy of your songs and leaving the envelope sealed until such time as you need to show proof. In this fantasy, the musician stands at the front of the courtroom, boldly displaying the date of the postmark. He then rips open the package to reveal his original lyric sheets, thereby proving his copyright.

The audience gasps. The perpetrator is lead away in handcuffs. The songwriter triumphs. This technique is purely a myth and will not work to protect anything. If you value your songs, spend thirty bucks a year and see that they are properly protected.

Recording A Demo

Musicians that intend to shop their songs to artists, compete for gigs, or otherwise distribute copies of their music, eventually need a "demo." A demo is simply an audio recording of a song. Back in the olden days (say…the '70's) that amounted to a reel to reel or cassette tape of the songwriter with his guitar, playing the chords and singing the melody. Today that simply won't do. We live in a time when the tools for audio recording are in the hands of even the most modest musicians. Typical demo tapes include full arrangements and top notch musicianship and production. If you want your song to compete, your demo will have to measure up.

The Songwriter's Demo

There are generally two different kinds of demos: a song demo, and an artist demo. As you might suspect, the song demo is designed to showcase a song, while an artist demo is designed to showcase a performer or group. When recording a song demo, there are some specific things you should consider that are different from an artist demo:

<u>First</u>, mix the vocals loud. Make sure all the lyrics are audible and understandable. It also never hurts if the vocal performance is phenomenal. If you don't have a great voice, hire someone that does.

<u>Next</u>, keep your intros, solos, and outros short. An artist considering your song wants to hear the song, not your skill as an instrumentalist or composer. When your song is in an industry insider's CD player, you have precious little time to impress them. Don't dawdle! Get to the chorus within forty-five seconds at most.

<u>Last</u>, it always pays to have your demo mastered so that its volume level is similar to commercially released CD's. It's embarrassing when your CD ends up in a tray next to someone else's and it sounds like a whisper.

Doing It Yourself

Because recording equipment has become so affordable in the last decade (mostly via digital audio and computer software), many songwriters and musicians are opting to record their own demos. This is a perfectly legitimate way to approach it as long as you understand that having groovy recording gear does not guarantee that you can produce great-sounding recordings. There is a huge learning curve attached to the recording process, one that takes many years to master.

Many musicians enjoy this process and are willing to tackle the challenge, but be careful—your home studio can have a detrimental effect on your songwriting. To show you what I mean, read the following article I wrote.

"Home Recording—
Lead Me Not Into Temptation"
December 6, 2009

Twenty years ago, who could have imagined a time when a person could write, arrange, record, duplicate, and distribute music to the entire world. We songwriters now live in an era of unprecedented creative freedom, with a wealth of capabilities and audio tools at our disposal. Why is it, then, that we can't finish a dang song?

Original Sin

We got into trouble, because like Eve in the Garden of Eden, we bit the apple without first reading the fine print. Our newly found knowledge and freedom has come with a price: we must now work for ourselves. Not only must we be songwriters, but producers, engineers, engineer's assistants, multi-instrumentalists, and bright-eyed interns willing to fetch coffee for free. We have to worry about mic placement, signal routing, monitoring schemes, levels, processing, and effects. Is it any wonder the creative energy needed for songwriting often gets burned figuring out why the new driver for the sound card isn't working?

The Sirens' Call

Audio recording is very seductive; maybe even downright sexy. Every day new plug-ins, soft-synths, gizmos, and widgets are introduced to tempt and delight. Songwriting today requires the self-control of a saint. Just as the mythical explorer Odysseus was lured by the Sirens, so many musicians are lured by lushly chorused walls of layered guitars and angelic, multi-tracked vocal harmonies…only to be dashed upon the rocks of an unfinished song.

Deliver Me From Evil

So how do we avoid these temptations? How do we ignore the wily serpent, or lash ourselves to the proverbial mast? How do we write good songs using today's technology? The answer is quite simple: we write good songs by making crappy recordings.

While writing, forget about all the things that make a good recording: finding a good guitar tone, setting your levels perfectly, capturing the best performance, or figuring out what the heck keeps squeaking in the background. Don't work out vocal harmonies. Don't experiment with instrumentation. Concentrate instead on getting your ideas into your computer as quickly as you can, and finding only the chords, melody, and lyrics.

Once the foundation of your song is built, you can begin to arrange it—try different harmonies and voicings, experiment with instrumentation, and develop the musical themes. All the concerns of making a great recording, however, should still be secondary.

Absolution

All who resist temptation while writing songs will find

themselves doubly blessed, for not only will their songs improve, but their recordings as well. With their songs already written, they will be free to try different microphones, and experiment with EQ settings and double-track guitars during the recording process, without killing the spontaneity of the songwriting process. They will be able to focus on capturing good performances without worrying that they will have to trash them later because they don't fit an adjustment that must be made to the song's basic form.

Such is the proper order of things.

Finis

The Audio Sketchpad

I like to draw. When I was young I drew all the time, mostly people. I always started with the face. I patiently worked through every detail: the eyes and eyelids, the nostrils, the mouth, all the lines and wrinkles. Once it was perfect, I moved to the neck and chest. Arms came next, and then hands. I made sure every detail was perfect before moving on. I continued in this manner until the entire person was drawn, and then I would sit back and scrutinize my masterpiece –a very detailed person with body parts that were hideously out of proportion.

Eventually I came to understand that the experienced artist works in a very different way. They begin their drawings with broad, light strokes, outlining just a basic shape. Unconcerned with detail, and thinking only of form, proportion, and perspective, they work the shape, gradually darkening their strokes and clarifying lines as they go. They work quickly, never concentrating on details at the expense of the whole.

Only after these larger challenges have been met do they begin to craft the smaller details, but still with an eye for the big picture. Once I understood this new way of working, I was able to create drawings that displayed a whole new level of artistry.

With the advent of computer-based recording, there are now recording studios in basements and bedrooms everywhere. Songwriters and musicians are experiencing an era of unprecedented creative freedom. But along with that freedom has come a price. As noted in my article above, 'Now, not only must we be songwriters and instrumentalists, but multi-instrumentalists, producers, engineers, and engineer's assistants.

As a musician in a professional recording studio, you are allowed to focus mainly on the songs and your performance. Others handle the tasks of recording such as mic placement, signal routing, monitoring schemes, levels, processing, and the like. In contrast, a songwriter in a home studio can find themselves so bogged down by such details that the creative energy needed for songwriting ends up buried beneath a mountain of patch cords. Before you start feeling like a first-grader with a pencil, remember that the same technology that has shackled us with all these extra duties has also given us something musicians have never had before: an audio sketch-pad.

But, just as I had to rethink the way I was using my pencils, learning to properly use an audio sketch pad requires a new way of looking at things. Mostly it requires the patience not to get ahead of yourself. Recording is very seductive. Just as the mythical explorer Odysseus was lured by the Sirens, so many musicians are lured by chorused walls of layered guitars and vocal harmonies, only to be dashed upon the rocks of an unfinished song. Say it once with me: begin with broad strokes.

Start by laying out your song's form. Forget about tone. Forget about levels. Forget about performance. Just record. Record as fast as you can and get your ideas into your computer so you can do something with them. Move audio clips around and rearrange them into an order that is interesting.

Songs can vary widely in their structure, and you must decide where the verses and choruses work in yours. Would two verses in a row sound better? Would an extra bar before the last chorus help to create tension? Where does the bridge work best - before the last verse or after? Use broad strokes. Move things around. Thinking only about the song as a whole, get the major pieces into place in a way that makes sense.

Once you are satisfied with the form of the song, you can take the time to try different vocal harmonies, flesh out the accompaniment, or look for ways to develop the theme and add some variety. Work out the parts for the various instruments so that they work well together. Don't second guess your song's form. Unless you are absolutely sure something needs to be changed, work forward not backward.

Now that your song's structure and arrangement have been worked out, and you have a solid form to build on, you are free to record "keeper" tracks without killing the spontaneity of the songwriting process. Take the time to find good mic positions and experiment with different vocal mics and EQ settings. Double-track guitars.

With the process of creative songwriting behind you, you are free to focus on creative recording. Now you can also focus on capturing a good performance without worrying that you will have to trash it later because it doesn't fit an adjustment that must be made to the song's basic form.

At some point, an artist needs to step back from his work to make a judgment about its progression as a whole. A painter uses distance. A musician uses time. You need to separate yourself from your song for a while so that you can approach it again with objectivity. Take a break. Let it sit for a day or two.

When you start on it again, don't immediately pick up where you left off. First listen to the song all the way through. Is there anything diminishing the song as a whole? Are there better choices that could be made? Make sure the most important elements of your song are the most important. Don't let instrumental solos or special effects ruin a beautiful melody.

Finally, bring the project to an end. Don't languish on one song forever. At some point you must decide you have done the best you can with your present level of musicianship, recording experience, and gear, and move on. Perhaps it's not your greatest work. Maybe you're sure you can still nail the guitar solo with just one more take. Get over it. A finished song in the hand is worth two in your computer. There are still too many other important songs waiting to be written. Sharpen your pencil and get back to work!

Using A Pro Studio

Most professional songwriters do not record their own demos. They turn to top-notch studios that specialize in it. There are some huge advantages to doing it this way. Most importantly, the level of musicianship is usually very high. Many of the big names you see in the credits of major albums are session players that could very well end up working on your song! These studios have access to big-time players and keep them on call. Unless you can say the same thing, using a pro studio is worth it for this reason alone!

Another huge advantage large studios have is their rooms. They are designed and constructed to create ideal acoustic spaces in which to record and mix music. A boxy bedroom or basement is the exact opposite! If such considerations seem superfluous to you, you owe it to yourself to visit a large studio some time. Stand in one of their rooms and just listen. It's pure ear-candy!

Because they record demos all the time, they can do it much more quickly than a typical studio session. If you booked a studio and brought in all your own instruments to record one song, an engineer may spend an entire day just getting everything mic'ed up and sounding good.

On the other hand, a demo studio usually has "house" drums and amplifiers that they keep mic'ed up all time and can complete your entire song in a single day. Obviously, the less studio time it takes to record your song, the cheaper it will be. A typical song demo from a studio like this usually runs between $250 and $700 depending on how many instruments you want in your arrangement. That is really a pretty good deal when you consider that it covers studio time, production costs, and some of the best musical talent around.

Pursuing Your Goals

I am a huge believer in goal setting, but I always stress that a dream is not a goal. To qualify as goals, the things you want to accomplish must be written down. Until you do this, they are merely wishes. I'm not just talking songwriting here... I'm talking life.

I've always kept such a list. Some of the things on my list are whimsical: bicycle along the Oregon coast, go parasailing in Mexico, go river rafting in Yellowstone. Others are more serious: own a home, write a book. Many more are personal goals that revolve around my wife and children. I continually add things I want to accomplish, and check off those goals I've achieved.

Take the time to make a list of the things that are important to you. Refer to your list often and work toward it every day. I firmly believe that if you do this, you will find a way to make those things a reality. Find a balance in your life that gives you the economic peace of mind that you need to be at your most creative.

Remember that music is all about emotional content. Pour your heart and all your unique experiences into your songs. Work hard to continually improve your craft.

Above all, remember these five words:

Music is its own reward.

Appendix

Internet Resources

www.tunesmith.net
www.justplainfolks.org
www.homerecording.com
www.americansongwriter.com

Song Contests

www.jlsc.com
www.songwriting.net
www.greatamericansong.com

Song Checklist

Lyrics

Are they "too clever"?
Do they make the title obvious?
Are they conversational? Do they sing well?
Does each verse cast its chorus in a new light?
Do they reveal the plot by degrees and resolve?
Do the first line and "launch lines" do their job?
Can you say anything better than you've said it?
Have you experimented with tense? Is it consistent?
Have you experimented with person? Is it consistent?

Music

Are the chords too complex?
Does the music suit the lyrics?
Have you chosen the best song form?
Are the hooks strong? Are there enough?
Is the melody built on short memorable phrases?
Does the music make it obvious where the title goes?
Is the melody linear, easy to sing, and in a normal vocal range?

Acknowledgement

The author would like to thank Larry Kolker for his valuable insight and assistance in preparing this book.

About the Author

Aaron Cheney is an award-winning songwriter, a guitarist, an artist, and an author. His songs run the gamut from country to heavy metal and have been recorded by artists across the country. His teaching experience includes courses in songwriting, music history, and music psychology.

www.ingramcontent.com/pod-product-compliance
Lightning Source LLC
LaVergne TN
LVHW061342060426
835512LV00016B/2633